WALKING UPSTREAM

Lloyd Ratzlaff

Thistledown Press

Thistledown Press Ltd.
UNIT 222, 220 20TH STREET W
SASKATOON, SK
S7M 0W9
WWW.THISTLEDOWNPRESS.COM

Library and Archives Canada Cataloguing in Publication

Title: Walking upstream / by Lloyd Ratzlaff.
Names: Ratzlaff, Lloyd, 1946- author
Identifiers: Canadiana (print) 20240536738 | Canadiana (ebook) 20240536746 |
ISBN 9781771872706 (softcover) | ISBN 9781771872737 (EPUB)
Subjects: LCGFT: Poetry.
Classification: LCC PS8585.A853 W35 2025 | DDC C811/.6—dc23

Edited by Elizabeth Philips
Cover and book design by Mark Byk
Printed and bound in Canada

Thistledown Press gratefully acknowledges the financial assistance of SK Arts, The
Canada Council for the Arts, and the Government of Canada for its publishing program.

For Shannon Faye
and
Sheri Carmen

I use not their tables, formulas, or schemes, rules and ways, for I have not learned from them. I have another teacher, which is the living fountain of nature.

— *Confessions of Jakob Böhme*, sixteenth-century shoemaker

CONTENTS

1
THE OLD PATH

Prismatic Lens

Full double rainbow on the river's brink,
and below, faint imprint
of a third.

I count the colours, not sure—
are there only seven?

Each rainbow arcs down to the water.
No hidden pots of gold there,
only a halcyon sun bending with the waves.

Pelicans float under the great crescent,
small white arks on the river.

Pica pica

I spy a human on the trail
and think, here comes another member
of the god species,
while over there, without divine concepts,
comes a magpie
who handily outflies us both.

Magpie, I love you more
for your flight and strut
than for your
squawk,
but can't vilify a creature
ten times tougher than I am
and a hell of a lot more handsome.

The Realm

A king abroad in my kingdom,
small domain on neighbourhood streets
but mighty big at the riverbank.

Neither crown prince
nor enchanted frog,
a monarch of no account
who likes to hide sometimes
in a copse of aspens
and listen.

In the Reeds

Red-winged and yellow-headed blackbirds
announce my arrival
at the edge of the marsh
where coots and pintails and mallards swim.

Hey hey,
whoever you are!

They light on the bulrushes' woollen heads
and sway against cloudbanks,
all reflected in the swamp's green water.
Hey you
mud hen in the reeds,
so near yet so hidden,
only the tinks on some tiny anvil
betray the place of your nesting.

[In the egg that hatches, an updraft. In the bird that flies, a stone.]

In My Childhood Village

The train came one day a week.
Some early evenings at the tracks
near my grandfather's house,
I called out like a town crier
the words on the sign:

WARNING!
PERSONS USING THIS CROSSING
DO SO AT THEIR OWN RISK!

But at night I wasn't so brave—
who knew what baleful creatures lurked
in the tunnel under the tracks?
And I crept past the sign
without warning the town,
hurried towards the gate
in Grandpa's sheltering hedge.

Good Friday

Rain and north wind scourge
the trees, and I'm
as ill with the flu as the old religion
wanted me to feel
for crucifying
Christ.

Not Romans or Jews,
but *you*, Little Sinner in the third bench,
especially you.

No Easter egg for you.

Billfold

What did I get as a kid
in 1955
for finding and returning Bill Hinz's wallet
with ID and a twenty-dollar bill inside?

Fifty cents
and a bite in the ass
from his German shepherd.

Sparrowsworth

Sparrow hits window
drops
into empty flowerpot.

God saw the little creature fall
and lets it lie, unruffled
by notions of resurrection.

Are not two sparrows sold for a farthing?
(St. Luke offers a discount: five
for two farthings.)

The first bee of spring
answers
by bumbling away.

Evangelist

When I was a boy,
a travelling evangelist told us how long
eternity lasts.

If a bird flies a thousand miles
from here to a far-off mountain,
picks up a pebble in its beak
and brings it back,
flies again and again, going
and returning, carrying little stones,
by the time the mountain is levelled there
and rebuilt here, eternity
will barely have begun, and still
we children without Jesus in our hearts
will be writhing in a lake of fire
and brimstone.

I'm old enough now to tell the evangelist
that if his bird totes that mountain back
from here to there and midway builds
a fresh peak of bird guano,
so long the preacher will stand upright
in a pulpit with his flappy bible—
heaven for him, maybe,
but enough of hell for me.

Of my four cheeks,
the top two he can slap,
the bottom two he can kiss.

Five Crows and a Hawk

Five crows harry a red-tailed hawk
whirling, circling
above the river.

Hawk flies on, pays them no heed,
catches a vertical wind shear
and hovers
between sundog
and sun.

Ruby and Finnegan

My dog Ruby pees on one end
of a fallen branch,
and her brother Finnegan
on the other,
so both north and south poles
are piss-ends of the stick.

Benched

What possesses me with the spirit
and quirks of old prophets?

It's the wind blowing pages
from a park bench where I sit,
leaving me with a pencil in one hand
and an unpeeled orange in the other.

My Quarrel with Yahweh

One thing I learned from
old Patriarch Jacob:
wrestling with God
ends in a draw.

You come away with a limp
and a new name,
but God's as anxious to
get away from you
as you from him,
changed, half-defeated,
and you can call him
whatever you like.

He's a night spirit.
The sun hurts his eyes.

[I'd like to take the old path, but can't find it anymore.
There's only the earth under my feet.]

2
THE IRRESISTIBLE FORCES

The Waters of March

These are not the warmest waters,
but must surely be among the fairest
in bearing away the filth of the world.

A prayer for the river, then.
May you carry off human refuse
without harming the fish in your flow
or the ducks on your rippled back.

Speaking Up

River never bluer than under an October sun.
Today a thousand terns wing silent and restless
above the water,
drop and float
a while, take off again—
why so muted when usually so shrill?

Crows on the grass hushed like the terns,
a quartet of magpies also,
as if all the birds
have taken a vow of silence.

But now one crow breaks out—
three caws and a great fluster,
and away.

Little Buddha

Beetle multicoloured like Joseph's coat
works the edge of the path,
mauve-and-silver wings
and a teal abdomen aimed my way.

It digs between cobbles
like an anteater,
anchored by six legs
but toiling so urgently
they slip on the stones.

Until the beetle turns, pokes into grasses,
climbs an emerald blade
and whirrs off,
thus come little Buddha
thus gone.

[I love the finch who sings loud enough
to disturb my meditation.]

This Is How You Move

South wind on north-flowing river.
Waves rise and fall,
and between two
irresistible forces
have nowhere to go.

Two naked pines lean together
in a long dance,
limbs entwined against the sky.

And this is how you move
without going
anywhere.

Emotional Behavioural Eating Drinking
Working Breathing Disorders

But magpie is perfectly ordered,
like the doe grazing beside a thicket
with magpie inspecting her
from shoulder to rump.

Val-dera-ha-ha-ha-ha-ha,
a nondisordered magpie on my back.

Instructions for FLOWER STAND Fold Type Natural
(A found poem)

Please understanding the natural wood likely to have the status
of distortion, damage or some cracks.

The wood will possibly have some status of cracks, rot, rust
and other phenomena if the wood with water and wet.

Please pay more attention to the product which will be broken
under the situation of flop down.

Please do not throw and cast it, in order to avoid injury and
damage to the goods.

Please surely do not use it for other purposes.

[Ah to be Yosemite Sam, blown to smithereens but back
under my hat when it's dusted off, pistols ready to raise me
from the ground.]

Finnegan

My pup Finnegan is manic.
He growls, sniffs at my crotch,
shakes the stuff from a pull toy,
nips my heels, tugs my pantlegs.

I play ball with him, pick him up
and sing to him
but he wriggles off,
and if I dare to resume writing
he barks, *Get back here!*

Before I notice, he's eaten half of Nietzsche's
Thus Spake Zarathustra
and a good hunk of Helen Luke's
Dark Wood to White Rose—
one a tome by a mad genius and
the other a Jungian treatise on Dante's universe.

He should be, like me,
as wise as he is foolish.

Supplication

If tonight
I could manifest a dream,
I would conjure a field of ten
thousand butterflies aloft
in no kind of formation,
to help me rethink the meaning
of symmetry.

Chickadee

Pelican hauls its bulk south
for the winter.

Chickadee stays on the prairie
singing from frozen branches
where I can't see it,
deedeedee (maybe one *dee* more).

Or flits between hedge and feeder
in a hardscrabble life of finding seeds
to be cracked and eaten
one at a time
and shat to the snowbank.

But chickadee never has the blues,
never needs a cane handed down from yonder wall.

[You have heard a Zen master say, *Walk like a mountain.*
But I tell you, *Grouse like a mountain,* then you've got something.]

One May Evening

Walking around Candle Crescent
I hear wind chimes from a porch.

A small orchestra improvises
a jazz suite for spring.

Moody themes,
tempos jangling,
melodies punctuated
by single tones,
and silences where the wind itself
pauses to listen.

Cobalt River

Why do I walk riverbank paths?

For magpie's graceful swoop
and faintly ridiculous hop.

For ten yellow goslings bobbing
behind their mother goose on a river
so blue it's cobalt.

For the porcupine up a tree, out on a limb
on a high summer night,
where I settle under a gibbous moon
and wait an hour
for the creature to scramble down
and off through the bush.

For the sycamore tree of childhood's
Sunday school pictures
which I climb to sing from its low branches,
Zacchaeus was a wee little man
and a wee little man was he.

For bushes that feed me buffaloberries as tart
as ever childhood's were,
for the caragana hedge that shoots brown pods at me
where I sit reading Keats, watching smoke
from Queen Elizabeth Power Station across the river
unfurl and re-form endless patterns on the sky.

For a student's poem blown by wind into the public domain:
  I dreamt as a child How life would be
  With my perfect Job
  In my perfect World
  How I'd be the king of it all
  And I would have things made
  Oh how life deceived me

But this morning
I walk for the bluejay who halts my stride,
gives me an earful,
lifts me from my skull
to prove how much bigger the world is
than a human mind.

Earth Dream

No fabled creatures
rose to meet me as I groped
ever farther down,
and only my small lantern illumined
stone staircases in the earth.

And I fled to ethers so rare and high
that invisible presences
frightened me back to where
Earth herself became the dream.

[I am quantum, see me leap. I am chameleon
taking on the colours of soul.]

3
TO GROUSE LIKE A MOUNTAIN

It Would Be Sad

Above the clover
a hundred dragonflies mate
in mid-air,
while one couple lies curled
tail-to-tail on the ground.

Until another dragon drops down and steals a partner,
and the two are airborne and fucking
before the one left below can bumble dizzily
down the path
and find a stalk to rest on.

It would be sad
if it weren't so funny.

In the Old-time Religion

Petting, pawing, intercoursing—
all were forbidden before marriage,
but permitted afterward
so long as they didn't lead
to fucking.

Saved sealed sanctuskyriefied
glorified bonafide bornagainified
holy hullabalujah.

Benediction

Thanks to the beauty
who danced beside me
until the alarm rang me up.
For her flavour and scent,
and the innocence
making her lovelier still,
for all she offered
that I couldn't take,
thanks, it's the thought that counts.

To this apple
no god prevents me from biting,
which tastes sweeter than
the snake said.

For every shade of blue from
midnight to magpie to
the river's sapphire shimmer
on a cold fall afternoon.

[Raven, if only I could fly and bank and land like you,
but not have to salvage the dead gopher I swerve to avoid
on my way home.]

Cuckoo

Mount a cuckoo clock on my headstone
with twelve hands pointing at the hours
and a door to spring open
whenever someone approaches.

Cuckoo cuckoo,
not especially who's cuckoo,
just a reminder—
cuckoo cuckoo
(clap when you want it to stop)
cuckoo cuckoo cuckoo…

Coffee at Starbucks

Waiting for Harv's Auto to change my tires,
watching people traverse the mall.

This beautiful,
repulsive,
aspiring,
sorry mass of humanity.

Pierced girls with boyfriends slouching along.
Like my god, like what are we like doing?
He said, like just give it a break, he's really like nice,
and like whatever. O god, I'm like seriously an idiot.

I myself was educated with foolscap and dunce hats,
but thought I had
learned how to like.

Mr. Speaker

The parliamentary speaker rarely speaks
but to call for order in a fractious
and ungoverned house,
presiding over warring children
who display what every teacher in the nation
labours to prevent.

Politicians button suits,
rise to their occasions
to browbeat and intimidate,
moving forward while backpedalling
as cronies shout down and pound out
the dishonourable members opposite,
with every remark deflected to the speaker
who sits silent.

And they unbutton themselves
and sit down.

Portrait: Winter in Saskatoon

Old woman leans into dumpster,
her bottom in the air,
plastic bag for a left wing
and cane for a beak.

[Sitting half lotus on the riverbank, dog shit on my sole,
ant crawls up my pantleg headed you know where.]

Shopping Cart

Pathetic creature,
loaded up, banged around
and left empty at curbside
for winds to drive away.

Ump

Old umpire's belly
nearly touches the catcher's back
where she crouches behind home plate
in this all-girl ballgame.

Ball one,
strike one,
wild swing,
hit and run and
safe on first.

Catcher squats,
old ump tucks himself
back in.

Confession

Big Banger spewing stars,
what can a firecracker say
to such unfathomableness?
Not much.

Grand Inquisitor,
the world hosts me,
I host the world.
That's it.

O Great Thatness,
is the world ever at peace
unless I am?

I believe in Gad,
Ged, Gid, God, Gud,
and sometimes Gyd.

Also in Raven the size of a Model T
and sounding like one too.

Against a Rosy Sky

Sunrise, bone cold
this minus-forty January morning.

Magpie does what he does any
summer's day,
shows off,
chatters from branch
to branch
against a rosy sky.

Well, what did I expect,
he's magpie,
and with every right
to be cheeky.

Others of the clan sit round and robust
in their bushes, and I think:
our people don't think
highly enough
of your people.

Prairie Cemetery

Autumn stillness,
poplar leaf drifts
towards my father's grave.

4
Afloat

Seeking

The gulls of Wanuskewin cry overhead
while a meadowlark sings from a fence post.

In the distance I hear the thunders approach.

Mosquitoes cannot bite the bronze bull,
his cock as low to the ground as his beard.

One thunder questions, another rolls a reply.
The bronze woman knows them by name,
and the name of the cloud peering low over her tipi.

A spatter of raindrops,
a scent of honey on the southern breeze.

Something flutters—what shall I name it?

Nirvana Big Rest Motel

Not there like Buddha,
but here like Yahweh
under these eaves, quieted
by a steady rain
while petunias sag
under the water's grey weight.

Here where I can do nothing
for my mother in her care home bed
but think,
look Mother,
I am because of you.

[My nest is never empty, fledged and flown children
forever in the old man's head, where they cannot be thought away.]

For Once I Saw the Worm

For once I saw the worm
my children tried to show me
long ago.

Fat green bobbin moving
section by section,
sniffing, sensing, spelling
ess and jay and dash,
rolling with the wind
towards a curb
three steps away.

Raven's Loft
(For Wayne)

Every May long weekend our *Fischenführer*
summons four men to the Churchill
to angle at the rapids below the bridge
a short truck ride from Missinipe
and the raven's loft where we stay.

These are the rules of the loft:
When you fish, fish.
When not, sleep or read,
eat, drink, be merry
as befits married men not on the prowl,
maybe letting off steam
but forever wishing the women well.

Sun for two minutes,
rainstorm for ten,
who knows if it won't snow within the hour?

Four men in a tub on the river,
one keeping a fire kindled in the loft,
a log at a time,
sometimes nodding off between lines
of a poem that wants to be written.

Bush rabbit lopes behind the cabin,
raven passes over the loft the other way.

Another rain squall comes,
goes. The fishermen pull walleye
from water into falling rain.
Or not, since fish (as Murphy's Law notes)
are either shallow or deep
or somewhere in between.

Goodbye Little Apartment
(For Ellen and Brent)

Goodbye last of the old fridges
that wouldn't defrost.
Goodbye contraption of an air conditioner
where I languished on the floor
for a week that summer of forty-degree heat.

Goodbye shabby carpet
on which my lover and I ate spaghetti dinners
and drank white wine.
Good riddance to sour landlords
who don't give a damn about leaky taps
or noisy neighbours,
but raise the rent twice a year.

Farewell bedroom where my daughters slept
most weekends of their adolescence,
my office when they left home
but too often also a storeroom for clutter
piled before guests arrived,
and hardly unpiled a week later.

Goodbye balcony above the river
helping one country boy live in the city
near water and trees and wild animals.

So long Katza, undisputed
feline neighbourhood queen
who strolled in and out of homes,
stayed while she liked,
or left with great dignity if required.

Goodbye apartment above
where beloved friends lived for a decade,
from which one night we four walked to the riverbank,
got three sheets to the wind,
played hide-and-seek till five in the morning,
where I hid so well the others gave up
and I had to seek for them. And when
we'd found each other again,
lay on our backs on a footbridge
where the creek meets the river,
passed around a mickey of cinnamon schnapps,
and looked into the stars.

Hoot

What can trigger a laugh
like a dabbling duck's ass
upright in a slough,
small bill underwater
knowing exactly
when it's time to head south?

Thanksgiving

Grey day, empty streets,
everyone home thanking
God, Krishna, Buddha,
Jesus, Mohammed,
or a Great Spirit.

Quite a babel,
all those voices,
with my own dubious thoughts
barging in.

Rain

Rain falling so hard, Mother,
the drops on the pavement stand vertical
to the thunder's attention.

A windstorm lashes them sideways.

The elements settle,
the drops become street dancers
as the last thunder cracks and rolls
to God knows where.

Mother, you taught me to pay attention,
fight the good fight,
finish the course,
stand up till I couldn't.
In the care home
you often remembered yesterday
but not the day before,
nor the long labours of childbearing and rearing,
and I can't say if this was tragedy or mercy.

In your dying you have become a new mother
and I a new child,
which only makes it harder to let you go.

[Even this small mind holds more than one galaxy.]

With the River

I walk on a spring afternoon at the edge of the city. The winter was long, and immense banks of snow are thawing and running down to the river, which is still frozen on its far side and on the nearer shoreline jumbled with heaps of ice. But the sun is warm, and I remove my jacket, tie the sleeves about my waist, and at a familiar spot turn onto a path above the river.

A small boat drifts midstream. She draws me along the slope to where the bank falls off steeply and brush grows thick below. Unhurrying, she turns her prow and a fulgent light gleams out, as if from a great ingot of snow that had unmoored her, perhaps, breaking from the bank, and she transports it now downriver.

Gradually, she comes on towards a stand of willow saplings hanging over the water below my lookout, then shifts again, and I see it was not snow but sunlight reflecting from the craft's metal hull that dazzled my eye. And in the midafternoon light I make out an emblem and see a ruby stripe shining from her side.

Now the vessel nudges the shoreline, then backs off, as if wilfully, turns slowly alongside the strand, nestles under the willows, and lies still.

I recall the little white house of childhood, my bed under the slope of the rafters which I imagined as a boat drifting into darkness and dreams to carry me away. If I could lie down in this vessel now, where might the river take us?

Below, the craft moves again gently at the stern, eases her prow into the current, begins floating towards a channel between the ice shards on this side and the frozen expanse beyond, then drives into a northeasterly breeze that ruffles the water where she goes.

I follow on the upper path as she sails below, and we travel side by side until she comes to open water. There, the ruby stripe shines once more as the boat swings back upstream to follow a bend in the river.

How easy she lies on the water. How simple the river is with her.

Acknowledgements

A near-octogenarian having a first poetry collection published must count as a miracle, and this is because of the ministrations of Elizabeth Philips and her colleagues at Thistledown Press. I'm deeply grateful to them and to others who (perhaps unknowingly) encouraged me towards poetry: Rita Bouvier, Gerald Hill, Lynda Monahan, Glen Sorestad, Miranda Pearson, Seán Virgo, Joan Thomas, Donna Call, Jill Thompson, and Bruce Wright.

A few of these poems first appeared as literary nonfictions in my previous books *The Crow Who Tampered with Time, Backwater Mystic Blues, Bindy's Moon,* and in the anthology *Apart: A Year of Pandemic Poetry and Prose.*

As always, thanks to Larraine who aids and goads my writing life, and to our Westies, Ruby and Finnegan, furred, unfallen angels who never stifle their yawns.

Lloyd Ratzlaff is a former minister, counsellor, and university lecturer, author of three books of literary nonfiction, and editor of an anthology of seniors' writings and a children's book. He was a finalist for three Saskatchewan Book Awards, won two Saskatchewan Writers' Guild literary nonfiction awards, and served on the boards of several writing organizations. He was a columnist for *Prairie Messenger Catholic Journal* through its final nineteen years of publication, and taught writing classes for Foundations Learning & Skills Saskatchewan, the Western Development Museum, and the University of Saskatchewan Certificate of Art and Design program. *Walking Upstream* is his first poetry collection. He lives in Saskatoon.